15236

92
Ei

Darby, Jean

Dwight D. Eisenhower

DATE DUE

MAR 30 1991			

DWIGHT D.
EISENHOWER

DWIGHT D. EISENHOWER

A Man Called Ike

Jean Darby

Lerner Publications Company • Minneapolis

Acknowledgments

The photographs in this book are reproduced through the courtesy of: pp. 1, 30, 34, 85, Library of Congress; pp. 2, 6, 12, 16, 22, 26, 28, 31, 38, 41, 42, 48, 57, 63, 69, 78, 81, 86, 94, Dwight D. Eisenhower Library; p. 9, Kansas State Historical Society, Topeka; p. 14, United States Naval Academy Archives; pp. 19, 62, United States Military Academy Archives; p. 32, MacArthur Memorial; pp. 35, 44, National Archives; pp. 46, 52, U.S. Coast Guard; p. 64, U.S. Army; pp. 65, 104, Dwight D. Eisenhower Library/U.S. Army; p. 72, Los Alamos National Laboratory; p. 74, National Republican Party; pp. 80, 83, Southdale-Hennepin Area Library; p. 82, Minnesota DFL Party; pp. 84, 96, Smithsonian Institution; pp. 89, 91, 92, Dwight D. Eisenhower Library/National Park Service; pp. 98, 103, Dwight D. Eisenhower Library/U.S. Navy; p. 101, U.S. Air Force.

Cover photographs courtesy of Dwight D. Eisenhower Library.

Maps on pages 43, 53, and 58-59 are by Laura Westlund.

LIBRARY OF CONGRESS CATALOGING-IN-PUBLICATION DATA

Darby, Jean.
    Dwight D. Eisenhower: A man called Ike / Jean Darby.
      p.   cm.
    Bibliography: p.
    Includes index.
    Summary: A biography of the commanding general of the Allied forces in Europe during World War II who became the thirty-fourth president of the United States.
    ISBN 0-8225-4900-X (lib. bdg.)
    1. Eisenhower, Dwight D. (Dwight David), 1890-1969—Juvenile literature. 2. Presidents—United States—Biography—Juvenile literature. 3. Generals—United States—Biography—Juvenile literature. [1. Eisenhower, Dwight D. (Dwight David), 1890-1969. 2. Presidents.] I. Title.
E836.D36   1989
973.921'092'4—dc19
[B]
[92]   88-37344
                                         CIP

15236

Manufactured in the United States of America   AC

1 2 3 4 5 6 7 8 9 10 99 98 97 96 95 94 93 92 91 90 89

Contents

Maps appear on pages 43, 53, and 58-59.

(Top): The Eisenhower family in 1902: (top row) Dwight, Edgar, Earl, Arthur, Roy; (bottom row) David, Milton, Ida. (Bottom): The family lived in this home in Abilene while Dwight was growing up.

ONE

A Boyhood in Abilene

1890-1911

*"We all learned a degree of the spirit of
service from Mother."*
—Edgar Eisenhower

"Whoa!" A lanky, blue-eyed boy pulled on the reins and his horse came to a stop at 223 Cottonwood Street. He jumped from the buggy and a puff of yellow Kansas dust curled up around him. The morning was already hot, so he moved quickly to fill his basket with vegetables. He gave his horse a pat, then hurried around to the back of the house. Dwight Eisenhower had started his rounds.

He knocked. Waited. Whistled and kicked the dirt. Finally the door opened a crack and a lady peeked out.

"Good morning, ma'am." Dwight was cheerful. "Do you need some vegetables today?"

Mrs. Jones tucked loose strands of hair back over her ear and stepped out on the porch. "What do you have that's good?"

"Corn, radishes, tomatoes, carrots," he said, as if it were the best crop in the world.

Mrs. Jones reached into the basket and took out an ear of corn. "Any worms?" she asked as she half-stripped it.

"No, ma'am," he said. He told her that an ear of corn cost one penny.

She shook her head and set the ripped-open ear aside. "How much for a pound of tomatoes?"

"Five cents, ma'am."

"Sorry, Dwight," she said. "Nothing today."

Dwight felt his temper rise. Why did that woman waste his time? Why did she look but not buy anything? He had to go to other houses, and there were chores waiting at home. All afternoon he knocked on doors and talked to women. Some were friendly, but others were cross at being disturbed.

As he turned the corner off Cottonwood Street, he saw boys playing baseball. He pulled his horse to a stop. "Look at that," he said as if the animal could understand. "That guy can't hit anything." Dwight pulled a blade of grass and stuck it between his teeth. "I could do better than that with one eye shut." But this afternoon he had vegetables to sell. His family needed money, and it was his job to sell the produce that came from their garden.

He worked until dusk, then turned his squeaky wagon around and drove back over the railroad tracks.

Dwight David Eisenhower was born in a cottage that was little more than a shack. The town was Denison, Texas; the date, October 14, 1890. He was the third son of David and Ida. Arthur and Edgar were his older brothers. Before Dwight was one year old, the family moved to Abilene, Kansas, where his mother gave birth to four more boys: Roy, Paul (who died in infancy), Earl, and Milton.

By the time the Eisenhowers moved to Abilene, the town had become a quiet community of about 4,000. It was no longer part of the "Wild West." Gunfights and knifings had disappeared. Saloon keepers who wore "diamonds as big as hickory nuts" had moved west. Armed cattle rustlers were part of the past.

These later citizens were peaceful, but the honor code of the Old West remained: hard work and honesty. Unemployment was unknown. Young children worked around the house, and 8-to-12-year-olds held jobs. Teenagers found regular employment. The city ran the school, but families took care of their own sick and elderly. There were few taxes and no government services. Citizens policed themselves. The only contact with the outside world was a train which brought manufactured goods from the East Coast.

Doctors, lawyers, and successful businessmen lived with their families on the north side of the railroad tracks. Dwight's family and others who did not have much money lived on

Abilene, Kansas, in the 1890s

the south side. As a small child, Dwight did not understand the difference between the neighborhoods. He was much older when he realized that his family was poor. He might not have noticed because the Eisenhowers were respected in the community. They paid their bills on time, read the Bible, and went to church.

Sometimes Dwight worked in the creamery where his father worked. He and his brothers also took care of chickens, ducks, pigs, rabbits, a horse, and two cows. They picked cherries, apples, pears, and grapes from their orchard. Their mother canned food as it came in season. She dried fruit in the attic and baked bread in a wood-burning stove. She was a happy person, quick to laugh. But she disciplined her boys and was determined that they would know how to work. She taught each of them to cook and to clean the house. But the boys were not always good.

One day when relatives were visiting, Dwight and Edgar began to scuffle in the yard. It was not just a little fight; they were rolling in the dirt and heads were banging on the ground. Their cousin was afraid the boys would be hurt. "Ida," she called, "come quick." The boy's mother looked, smiled—and did nothing.

"Aren't you going to stop it?" the visitor asked.

"They have got to get it out of their system," Ida replied. "You can't keep healthy boys from scrapping. It isn't good to interfere too much."

When the fight was over, the boys thought more of each other than they had before. When they fought with outsiders, they stood together.

After school one day, Dwight was pushed into a fight with Wesley Merrifield. Wesley was bigger than Dwight, but Dwight was stubborn. A crowd gathered to watch the "toughest kid fight Abilene had ever seen." It lasted more than an hour. Finally Wesley gasped, "I can't lick you." Dwight rolled on the ground. "And I can't lick you." When they quit, both boys had bloody noses, cut lips, and battered ears. Their eyes were nearly swollen shut.

It was true that Dwight had inherited his father's temper. One Halloween night, his parents gave Edgar and Arthur permission to go trick-or-treating. Dwight begged to go along, but his father told him he was too young. Dwight's heart banged in his chest and his face grew red. Filled with anger, he ran out of the house, slammed the door, and pounded his fists against the trunk of an apple tree. He cried and hit the tree until his fists were a bleeding mass of torn flesh. Exasperated, his father grabbed him by the shoulders and shook him until he gained control of himself.

Dwight went to his room and cried into his pillow. After a while, his mother came to sit beside him. She put salve on his hands and bandaged them. After what seemed a long time, she said, "He that conquereth his own soul is greater than he who taketh a city." Later Dwight wrote, "I have always looked back on that conversation as one of the most valuable moments of my life."

Growing up, Dwight's nickname became Ike. He was not only known for his ability to fight, but he was also admired by his peers for his sense of fair play. As he grew, his smile became a part of his personality that people never forgot. He was good at hunting, fishing, cooking, and card playing. He studied history and read military books, learning how famous battles were fought. Schoolwork was easy, and sports were his favorite pastime. After sports came work, studies, and girls.

During his freshman year in high school, Ike fell and

As a boy, Ike loved sports and played on the Abilene High School baseball team. Ike is second from the right in the top row.

scraped his knee. Infection set in and he became delirious. His parents called Dr. Conklin, but there were no drugs like penicillin or sulfa in those days, so the red marks which marked the infection spread. Day after day, Ike slipped into and out of a coma while his mother held his hand or bathed his head. Every morning the doctor swabbed the sore with carbolic acid, but the medicine could not stop the red streaks from traveling up his leg and into his groin.

One day Ike woke up enough to hear Dr. Conklin say, "That leg will have to come off." Frightened, Ike called Edgar. "Look, Ed," he said, "they are talking about taking my leg off. I want you to see that they do not do it, because I would rather die than to lose my leg."

Edgar promised to stand watch. He never left his brother's side. Dr. Conklin could not persuade Edgar, or David and Ida, to let him amputate. He called their behavior "murder," but by the end of the second week, Ike's fever began to go down. The red streaks disappeared. Ike was going to recover.

In May 1909, Dwight and Edgar graduated from high school. Edgar wanted to go to the University of Michigan to study law, but his father believed that a lawyer could not be an honest man, and he refused to help Edgar pay for college. Dwight and Edgar devised a plan. They agreed that Edgar would go to college the first year. Ike would work and send him money. The second year, they would change places.

In September Edgar enrolled in school. For some unexplained reason, he stayed two years instead of one. During this time, Ike became close friends with Everett "Swede" Hazlett, who had attended high school with Ike. Swede was drawn to Ike from the beginning. "I liked him most for his sterling qualities," he said. "He was calm, frank, laconic and sensible, and not in the least affected by being the school hero."

One day Swede told Ike that he was going to attend the United States Naval Academy at Annapolis, Maryland. "My education will be free," he said. "The government will pay for it." To get into the Naval Academy at Annapolis or the U.S. Military Academy at West Point, New York, a person had to be appointed by a U.S. senator.

The idea of a free education appealed to Ike. He had no specific career in mind, but he knew he wanted to go to college. With Swede's encouragement, Ike began to work on a plan to get an appointment to the Academy. If Swede can do it, he thought, so can I.

Everett "Swede" Hazlett convinced Eisenhower to apply to the U.S. Military Academy at West Point. The two men met in high school and remained close friends throughout their lives.

He wrote to Senator Joseph Bristow, because he knew the senator would be choosing one candidate.

"I have graduated from high school and will be nineteen years of age this fall.

"If you find it possible to appoint me to one of these schools [Annapolis or West Point], your kindness will certainly be appreciated by me.

"Trusting to hear from you, concerning this matter, at your earliest convenience, I am respectfully yours,

"Dwight Eisenhower"

His letter went unanswered, but there was hope. One day while browsing through the newspaper, Dwight read that on October 4 and 5, competitive examinations would be given to applicants for the Military Academy at West Point and the Naval Academy at Annapolis. Quickly he wrote another letter to the senator. "Now, if you find it impossible to give me an appointment outright to one of those places, would I have the right to enter this competitive examination?"

This time Bristow answered. Of course Dwight had the right to take the test. Dwight studied long hours every day. His work paid off when he scored second out of a group of eight. Eisenhower was one year too old to enter Annapolis, so Bristow appointed him to West Point.

He left for school early one morning in June of 1911. Goodbyes were dignified. His father had already gone to work. His mother waved from their porch and he shook hands with his brothers.

Ike stood outside the railroad station, six feet tall and with broad shoulders and rock-hard muscles. He was self-confident and had an active, curious mind. He knew he was ready for a challenge.

The train puffed into the station and screeched to a stop. Ike took a final look at Abilene, then climbed into the third car. "All aboard," the conductor called. The train lurched and moved forward. It picked up speed and soon it was rumbling over the Kansas plains. As it traveled through small towns, children waved and their parents stood to watch the cars roll by.

No one knew the young man smiling through the window would one day be the world's most famous soldier—nor did the young man know it himself.

Eisenhower in his cadet uniform

∽ TWO ∽

West Point

1911-1915

*"It was no surprise to find him generally
liked and admired."*
—Swede Hazlett, speaking of Eisenhower

"Get your shoulders back! Suck in your stomachs! More! More! Hold up your head! Drag in your chin! Hurry!" The plebes (new West Point cadets) moved quickly from building to building as they turned in their money, received their uniforms, collected their bedding, and moved into their rooms at Beast Barracks. Dwight "Ike" Eisenhower was assigned to room 2644. Today a bronze plaque on the wall says, "This room was occupied by President Dwight D. Eisenhower, class of 1915, during his Fourth Class Year." (Fourth means the first year at the Academy.)

Yearlings (upperclassmen) called the plebes "Mr. Dumjohn" or "Mr. Dumgard." Plebes could not move fast enough. They were not treated as they had been at home. They were put down, embarrassed, and called stupid. Hazing (initiating new cadets by harrassing them) was rough.

Yearlings made plebes stand at attention for long periods of time. They made them pick up ants one by one until all the ants in a hill were gone. Plebes were made to recite nonsensical stories. The cadets had to hold clubs at arm's length until their muscles ached.

Some of them cried. They could not take the harsh treatment. Some left the Academy. But Ike did not weaken or lose his temper. When confronted by a barking, red-faced yearling, Ike reminded himself that he was getting a free education. Then he'd smile and know everything was going to be all right.

Ike paid more attention to the serious side of West Point. Its ceremonies sparked his feelings of patriotism. He clung to its traditions. He respected its sense of duty and service. He wanted to be part of the Long Gray Line (the cadets). He knew this even more when he stood on the parade ground and listened to the beat of the military band. The Corps was in full dress uniform and it marched in perfect rhythm. The United States flag waved.

When Eisenhower took the oath of allegiance, the words "United States of America" took on a new meaning for him. He knew that from then on, he would serve his country, not himself.

Instructors at West Point believed the Academy's duty was to instill respect for the past in students. Cadets were told about General Ulysses S. Grant and shown the room he once occupied. They were told, "General Lee slept here. Sherman there." Eisenhower, who loved military history, responded enthusiastically. He liked to wander about the plain, climb the cliffs, look down on the Hudson River, and reflect on the American Revolution. He often wondered what might have happened if Benedict Arnold, a revolutionary

Although life at West Point could be hard, Ike loved the Academy's sense of history.

war traitor who was in command of West Point in 1780, had surrendered the fort to the British.

Life was inspiring at the Academy, but it was also severe. Rooms were cold in winter and hot in summer. Food was unappetizing. Lessons were monotonous. Every day, in every class, cadets were expected to recite and give correct answers to questions. Many of the instructors were not well educated. Sometimes they did not know as much as their students. One day Ike was told to solve a difficult calculus problem. He found the answer in a shorter and simpler way than his instructor had. The instructor accused Ike of cheating by memorizing the answer.

Eisenhower was angry. He stood his ground. He had not cheated. He protested. He was in danger of being expelled from school when the head of the Mathematics Department stepped in. "I understand what you did," he said. "From now on we will teach that problem your way."

Sometimes Ike made serious mistakes. Though he liked

the Academy, he often thought its rules were too strict. One of his rebellious acts was to smoke. Cigarettes were forbidden at West Point, but Eisenhower smoked hand-rolled Bull Durhams. His roommate did not approve and his friends worried; he smoked anyway. When caught, he accepted his punishment, but even this did not stop him. He kept smoking.

Ike also would not keep his room neat. He was often late to formation. Sometimes he did not dress properly. One time a cadet corporal ordered Ike and another cadet to report to his room in "full-dress coats." He meant for them to come in complete uniform. The two plebes decided to do exactly as ordered.

"Atten-tion," the corporal shouted when they entered the room.

"Yes, sir." The plebes whisked open their coats, revealing their naked bodies.

The corporal turned red. "Return in complete uniform including rifles and crossbelts and if you miss a single item I'll have you down here every night for a week."

Football was important to Ike. He played hard, and during a game against Tufts University, he twisted his knee. Later that week, he hurt his knee again during a drill. The cartilage and tendons were severely torn. The doctor put his leg in a cast; the pain was so intense that Ike could not sleep. Worse than the pain was the knowledge that his days of playing football were over. There was even talk of his not receiving a commission in the army. He became depressed. His grades went down. He thought of resigning from the Academy.

A trip back home helped to change his mind. He was Abilene's hero. His family loved him. Even Wesley Merrifield said he "looked like a million dollars."

Back at West Point, Eisenhower was learning how to handle a rifle and small artillery. He practiced horseback riding and studied ways to build a bridge. By the time he graduated, he knew mathematics, geography, physics, and chemistry. He learned that a good officer is highly motivated and dedicates his life to his country. He understood that a good officer is an unselfish team player who is physically and emotionally courageous.

Eisenhower's class of 1915 became the most famous in West Point's history. In 1915, 164 men graduated. Of the 164, 59 became brigadier generals or higher. Three rose to the rank of full general, and two to the rank of general of the army. It was called "the class the stars fell on." Dwight D. Eisenhower would become the brightest star of all.

Dwight and Mamie on their wedding day, July 1, 1916

✑ THREE ✑

A New Life

1915-1935

"I have only asked to be allowed to go into battle."
—Dwight D. Eisenhower

Eisenhower graduated from West Point on June 12, 1915, and was accepted into the Infantry. He was stationed at Fort Sam Houston, outside San Antonio, Texas. One afternoon in October, he put on his pressed uniform and brightly polished boots. He looked at himself in the mirror, approved of his strong, athletic physique, then walked out of the Bachelor Officers' Quarters, where he lived. He was on his way to make an inspection of the guard posts when Major Hunter Harris's wife called to him. "Ike, won't you come over here? I have some people I'd like you to meet." A small group of military personnel was lounging in yard furniture.

"Sorry," Ike called back. "I'm on guard and have to start an inspection trip."

"Humph!" Mrs. Harris muttered. "There goes the woman-hater of the post." Then she called, "We didn't ask you to come over to *stay.* Just come over here and meet these friends of mine."

Unable to get away without seeming rude, Ike stepped off the curb and went to meet them.

"Good day," he smiled. He was glad he stopped. He could scarcely hear what Mrs. Harris was saying, his thoughts were so surprising. *She's beautiful. Who is she?* Then he heard her name: Mamie Doud.

"Happy to meet you, Mamie."

While he was thinking *she's beautiful,* she was having her own thoughts: *He's the handsomest male I've ever seen.*

The following day she was still thinking about Ike when the telephone rang. "Miss Doud?" Ike asked. He invited her to go dancing. "Tomorrow?" Mamie was surprised. Ike called the next day and the next. Mamie was always busy, but Ike was determined. "Four weeks from today," he said. "May I see you four weeks from today?"

"Of course," Mamie smiled and marked her calendar.

On Valentine's Day, 1916, Mary Geneva Doud (Mamie) accepted Ike's West Point ring to mark their engagement. They were married on July 1 that year.

Their three rooms in the BOQ (Bachelor Officers' Quarters) were not like the home Mamie had come from. Her father was a wealthy meat-packing business owner. She had lived in a beautiful house with servants to cook and clean.

But Mamie was in love and anxious to be a good wife. Besides keeping their apartment clean, she taught Ike social graces that he had not learned in the small town of Abilene.

Mamie knew how to give parties, and the Eisenhowers liked to entertain their friends. They played cards, listened to music, and sang. Their apartment soon became known as "Club Eisenhower."

Meanwhile, World War I had begun in Europe in 1914. German troops had moved across the Belgian border. The British and French had come to Belgium's aid. France was asking for the Russians to help. Most European nations entered the war. No one was saying what the United States would do. But on May 7, 1915, a tragedy in the North Atlantic Ocean made it clear that the U.S. would soon be drawn into the conflict.

A German submarine lurking beneath the ocean's surface sank the British passenger liner *Lusitania*. Nearly 2,000 lives were lost. More than 100 of them were Americans. Anger flared. U.S. citizens would not tolerate such actions. War drew nearer.

The war in Europe grew worse when Germany announced that its submarines would sink all vessels going into or out of Allied ports. Germany hoped for a quick victory while the United States was still at peace. But this was not what happened.

President Woodrow Wilson asked Congress for a declaration of war. "It is a fearful thing to lead this great, peaceful people into war, into the most terrible and disastrous of all wars.... But the right is more precious than peace, and we shall fight for the things which we have always carried nearest our hearts—for democracy." It was April 2, 1917.

Excitement ran high among the servicemen. Fear lodged in the hearts of their wives. No one knew what the war would bring. But Ike wanted to be part of it. He had gone to West Point to become an officer. He had been trained to fight. He belonged on the front line—or so he thought.

The army had another plan. Eisenhower was promoted to captain, then sent to Fort Oglethorpe, Georgia, to train officers and candidates. He did not like his assignment and began to pester the War Department to send him overseas.

"Ike," a superior officer told him. "Stop asking."

"Sir," Ike said, "I have only asked to be allowed to go into battle."

There was one bright spot in Ike's life. Mamie gave birth to their first son on September 24, 1917. They named him Doud Dwight and called him "Icky." Ike and Mamie were thrilled with their little boy. "He's perfect," Mamie said. Ike agreed.

Even though Ike did not like his assignment, he impressed officers and trainees alike. "Our new Captain," a

The Eisenhowers' first son, Doud Dwight, was born in 1917. The happy parents nicknamed the boy "Icky."

trainee wrote, "is, I believe, one of the most efficient and best Army officers in the country.... He gets the fellows' imaginations worked up and hollers and yells and makes us shout and stomp until we go tearing into the air as if we meant business."

Throughout the year, Eisenhower completed new assignments, in Fort Leavenworth, Kansas, Camp Meade, Maryland, and Camp Colt in Gettysburg, Pennsylvania.

Promotions came quickly. By October 14, 1918, Ike was a lieutenant colonel. Along with his new rank came orders for overseas duty. He was going to France. But on November 11, 1918, the Germans signed the Armistice, which ended World War I. Ike had missed the fighting and his rank was soon returned to major. He was disappointed.

A businessman from Indiana offered Ike a position in his firm. "It will pay much more than you make in the army," he said.

But Ike could not accept his offer. He wanted to serve his country. "I'll stay in the army," he said. "There will be another war. I want to be part of it."

While working with tanks at Camp Meade, Eisenhower met George S. Patton, Jr. Patton was dramatic and outspoken. Ike liked him—he thought Patton was reckless and fascinating.

Eisenhower and Patton were both students and instructors at the Infantry Tank School. Each commanded a battalion of tanks.

They were excited about their work. They published articles about tank warfare. "The clumsy, awkward and snail-like progress of the old tanks must be forgotten; in their place

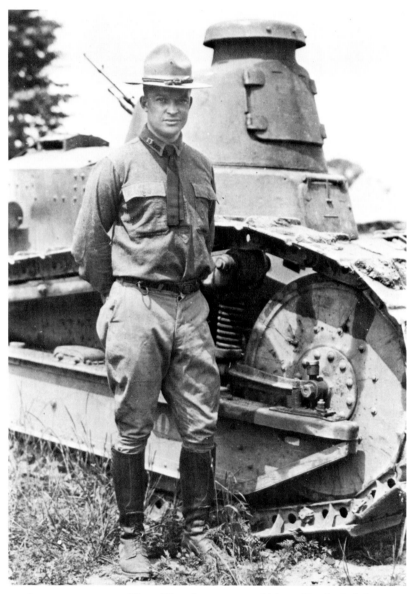

As a young army officer, Eisenhower proved himself to be bright,
hardworking—and ahead of his time. He believed in using tanks
in warfare, years before the army realized the wisdom of his ideas.

we must picture this speedy, reliable and efficient engine of destruction," Eisenhower wrote in an article.

The War Department chided Eisenhower, saying his ideas were not only wrong but dangerous. He was to keep them to himself. Ike did as he was told. It was not like him to struggle against the entire U.S. Army.

In the fall of 1920, he met another man who had a great influence on his life: General Fox Conner. Eisenhower knew him by reputation. Conner was known as one of the smartest men in the army.

Conner asked Eisenhower and Patton to show him their tanks. After inspecting the iron monsters, Conner asked how the machines could be used as future weapons. Eisenhower and Patton showed Conner around Camp Meade. They explained how tanks could be important in the next war. After Conner returned to Washington, he praised them for their work and told them to keep at it.

Soon after that, Conner was assigned to Panama to command an infantry brigade. He asked Eisenhower to join him as his executive officer. Ike was anxious to go with Conner. He thought the transfer would be routine, but once again, he met with disappointment. When he asked his commanding general, Samuel Rockenbach, for a transfer, Rockenbach told Eisenhower he could not spare him.

Eisenhower felt that he was getting nowhere in his career, but his family life was warm and happy. He and Mamie enjoyed each other, the army social scene, and their three-year-old son. In December, however, their lives took another turn for the worse.

Ike put up a Christmas tree and Mamie decorated it. A week before Christmas, Icky came down with scarlet fever. On the second of January, 1921, he fell into a deep sleep—

Fox Conner was an important figure in the army after World War I. He became Eisenhower's teacher and mentor.

and then he was gone. Ike said that the death of his son was the greatest disaster of his life. For the rest of his life, he sent flowers to Mamie every year on Icky's birthday. Today Icky's remains lie beside those of his mother and father in Abilene, Kansas.

At the end of the fall, General John J. Pershing became chief of staff of the army. He was fond of General Fox Conner, and Conner still wanted Ike as his executive officer in the Panama Canal Zone. Pershing gave the orders for Eisenhower to go to Panama. Mamie and Ike packed, said goodbye to friends, and took off for their first foreign military service. They arrived in Panama in January 1922.

These were happy months for the Eisenhowers. Ike studied long hours and learned much from Conner. Together they pored over maps and discussed battles. "Prepare for war," Conner told him. "Another war is coming." Ike believed the general. When another war came, he wanted to be ready.

Ike was feeling better about his career, and life was good to the Eisenhowers in another way. Their second son, John Sheldon Doud Eisenhower, was born on August 3, 1922.

The Eisenhowers' tour of duty ended in Panama in the fall of 1924. New orders took them to many different places: first Camp Meade, where Ike coached football, then Colorado for recruiting duty. Next, at the army's prestigious and difficult Command and General Staff School at Leavenworth, Ike graduated first in his class. He then moved to Washington, D.C., where he wrote a guide to the American battlefields of Europe; then on to the Army War College, at Fort McNair (also in Washington). After Fort McNair, the Eisenhowers lived in Paris, France, for about a year. They came back to Washington, D.C., in November 1929. There Eisenhower worked in the office of the Assistant Secretary of War.

The Eisenhowers met for a reunion in Abilene in 1925. From the left are Roy, Arthur, Earl, Edgar, David, Milton, and Ida; Ike is sitting in front.

General Douglas MacArthur was chief of staff of the U.S. army from 1931 to 1935 and Eisenhower's boss for seven years. The two men were very different and sometimes argued.

Franklin D. Roosevelt became president in March, 1933, while the U.S. was in the midst of the Great Depression. But Washington was a prosperous city. Business boomed. Government officials lived well. Office buildings were being built for Roosevelt's many new bureaucrats.

On Sundays Ike put on his derby hat and striped pants. Then the Eisenhowers climbed into their Buick and paid courtesy calls on superior officers. His son John said, "This was a chore that Dad detested and he made little secret of it."

Eisenhower's Washington tour ended six years later. In 1935 General Douglas MacArthur, who had become chief of staff of the army in 1931, wanted Ike as his assistant in the Philippines. Ike had become MacArthur's personal assistant in 1932. MacArthur admired Eisenhower's devotion to duty, mastery of detail, loyalty, and efficiency.

Ike was unhappy about the move. Mamie refused to go. It was General MacArthur and a lonely Major Eisenhower who boarded the train headed for the San Francisco harbor, bound for Manila.

✂ FOUR ✂

The Coming of War

1936-1943

"I belonged with troops; with them I was happy."
—Dwight D. Eisenhower

Mamie and John Eisenhower sailed for Manila after John graduated from the eighth grade in 1936. Mamie was unhappy with the move and even more unhappy with the Philippines. Her first shock came when she saw her husband.

"What have you done?" she gasped when he took off his hat.

He didn't have to answer. He had shaved his head. "I did it to keep cool," he told her.

It was hot in Manila and their apartment was not air-conditioned. Bugs scampered across the floor, into cupboards, and up the walls. At night the family slept under nets to keep out mosquitoes. During the day, window shutters were closed to keep out the sun. Mamie was ill, and Ike did not get along well with MacArthur.

"Why don't you fire me?" Ike pounded his fist on the desk and shouted at the general.

The Nazi party started in Germany in the 1920s and gained strength during the 1930s. Led by Adolf Hitler (shown here seventh from left in the front row), the Nazis ruled Germany from 1933 to 1945.

Adolf Hitler was Germany's dictator from 1933 to 1945. He led the country into World War II.

This was impossible. MacArthur needed Eisenhower. In a letter to Ike, he thanked him for his "cheerful and efficient devotion."

In 1936 Ike was promoted to lieutenant colonel. In 1939 Conner's prediction of another war came true. German aircraft, tanks, and motorized troops attacked Poland. It was the beginning of World War II.

After the fall of Poland, German armies rolled across Europe and crushed six more countries: Denmark, Norway, Belgium, Luxembourg, the Netherlands, and France. Ike thought Adolf Hitler was power-drunk and insane.

Adolf Hitler ruled Germany from 1933 to 1945 and turned the country into a powerful war machine. He was one of the cruelest leaders in world history, spreading death as no one had ever done before. "Close your eyes to pity! Act brutally!" he told his soldiers and members of the Nazi party, the political party he led.

Hitler hated Jewish people and blamed Germany's problems on Jews. He built concentration camps where about six million Jews and millions of other people were murdered.

Patton wrote to Eisenhower, "hoping we are together in a long and BLOODY war."

Ike didn't agree. The thought of terrible battles pained him. He didn't like to think of losing men. In a letter to his brother Milton, Ike wrote, "It's a sad day for Europe and for the whole civilized world. . . ." He smashed his cigarette in a glass dish. "But," he said to himself, "if we're going to get into it. . ." He couldn't finish. He had been left out of the last war. It wouldn't happen again if he could help it.

Finally orders came to leave the Philippines. "Mamie," he called, "we're going home."

John was on his way to West Point. Ike and Mamie were going to Fort Lewis in Washington state.

After they were settled, Ike wrote to his friend Omar Bradley. "I'm having the time of my life. Like everyone else in the army, we're up to our necks in work and in problems, big and little. But this work is fun! . . . I could not conceive of a better job."

Ike walked with a bounce, his eyes darting, missing nothing. Wherever he went, he talked and asked questions. He told anyone who would listen that the army needed strong, tough, efficient, hardworking officers. He didn't think the United States could stay out of the war in Europe. Because of his views, he earned the nickname "Alarmist Ike." He worked hard and hoped for an assignment overseas. But in November 1940, he received a telegram from Leonard

Gerow, chief of the War Plans Division in the War Department. The message made his worst fears a reality. It said: "I need you in War Plans."

The worst thing possible was happening again! He was going to miss the fighting at the front. The thought of being stuck behind a desk upset Ike so much that he broke out with shingles. From his bed, he wrote to General Gerow: "Your telegram sent me into a tailspin. Given a choice, I would rather stay with troops."

This time Ike had his way. Now a full colonel, he stayed with the troops and went on field maneuvers in Louisiana. The maneuvers were the largest held by the U.S. Army before the U.S. entered the war. "All the old-timers here," he wrote, "say we are going into an [awful] spot, to live with mud, malaria, mosquitoes and misery. But I like to go to the field, so I'm not much concerned about it."

The officers liked Ike's good humor and they liked the way he worked. But most of all, they admired his ability to lead. One of his leadership strengths was that he listened to the soldiers' troubles. Newspaper reporters were also beginning to take note of Ike.

On Sunday, December 7, 1941, Japanese aircraft flew over Hawaii and dropped bombs on Pearl Harbor. The United States, Canada, and Great Britain declared war on Japan on December 8, 1941. Four days later, Germany and Italy declared war on the United States, and the United States declared war on Germany and Italy. On November 30, Soviet troops had invaded Finland. Now it seemed the whole world was at war.

General George C. Marshall, who was army chief of

Eisenhower meets with George C. Marshall in Algeria in 1943. Marshall and Eisenhower respected and liked one another very much.

staff, sent for Eisenhower. He told Eisenhower about the situation in the Pacific; the Japanese would likely attack the Philippines. Then he leaned across his desk, knitted his eyebrows, and asked, "What should be our line of action?"

Eisenhower asked for a few hours to think about it. When he returned, he said, "We dare not fail. We must take great risks and spend any amount of money required."

Marshall agreed. "Do your best to save the Philippines." He put Eisenhower in charge of the Far Eastern Section of the War Plans Division.

This new task was difficult. Reinforcements had to be sent to the South Pacific. But there were no reinforcements to send. Ships were needed to transport supplies. But there were not enough ships. "Ships! Ships! All we need is ships!" Eisenhower wrote in his diary in January. As an afterthought, he added, "Also ammunition, anti-aircraft guns, tanks, airplanes, what a headache!"

Eisenhower was angry with MacArthur and he was angry with the commander of the United States Navy, Admiral Ernest J. King. He thought they wouldn't cooperate, wouldn't work for the good of everyone, and considered only themselves. MacArthur was angry as well because he wasn't getting the supplies he needed to defend the Philippines against the Japanese.

With every day that passed, Marshall admired Eisenhower more. His skill in working with people led him beyond the Pacific into problems around the world. He met with European leaders. He believed the British were difficult and arrogant. But as he worked with them his smooth leadership style began to surface. He was led to write: "In a war such as this, when high command invariably involves a president, a prime minister, six chiefs of staff, and a horde of lesser 'planners,' there has got to be a lot of patience—no one person can be a Napoleon or a Caesar." His abilities brought him another promotion. On March 27, 1942, he became Major General Eisenhower.

Now a general with two stars, Eisenhower was put to work drafting plans for the first offensive in Europe. "We've got to keep Russia in the war and hold India," he said. "Then we can get ready to crack Germany through England." By late March, Eisenhower and his staff had made a specific plan. President Roosevelt approved the plan, and Ike flew to London to share his idea with the British. After six days of arguing, the British accepted his plan.

Eisenhower sent messages to Admiral King, asking for the navy's support. But the admiral was stubborn. "I cannot spare ships," he told Eisenhower. "I have no extra landing craft."

Eisenhower fought for what he believed. He wanted to gather thousands of soldiers, infantrymen, paratroopers, tank divisions, and airplanes. The code name for the buildup was "Bolero."

Then came more trouble. The president decided to send troops to Australia. There weren't enough transport ships or landing craft. There weren't enough men to send to the Pacific and to England. The U.S. had not prepared for war. In disgust Ike wrote, "The actual fact is that not one man in twenty in the [government]...realizes what a grisly, dirty, tough business we are in."

But Ike continued to strive, to plan, and to work well with temperamental heads of government and armies. His excellent performance paid off, and on June 11, 1942, Marshall appointed him commander of the European theater of operations. Ike was in the war at last!

On June 24, 1942, Eisenhower arrived in England. As head of the armed forces he was a VIP (Very Important Person). Right from the start, people admired Ike's ability to communicate with heads of government and soldiers. His nickname was appealing. He used expressions like "big operator," "I told him to go peddle his papers," and "Big Shots." He referred to "my old home town, Abilene," and described himself as "a simple country boy." He sometimes responded to questions with, "That's just too complicated for a dumb bunny like me." His smile was his trademark. An Irishwoman, Kay Summersby, became his driver, and Telek, a small Scottie pup, his pet. Eisenhower spent weekends at a country house which he named Telegraph Cottage.

In spite of Ike's popularity, his position was difficult. One

When Ike lived in England as commander of the European theater of operations, he had little time to relax. But when he could he spent weekends at Telegraph Cottage, where he golfed, played bridge, and read Western novels — his favorite kind of book.

of his first tasks was to improve the image of American soldiers in England. The British had little good to say about them. A popular British saying called the Americans "overpaid, oversexed, overfed, and over here."

Another problem was the way the war was going in the Soviet Union. The Germans had invaded and the Soviets were running low on supplies. Joseph Goebbels, the Nazi Minister for Propaganda, wrote: "We have received a report from a deserter in Leningrad, according to which conditions there must be simply catastrophic...."

The knowledge that the Soviet Union might be nearing collapse frightened Eisenhower. He said over and over, "We must keep Russia in the war." The United States and Britain sent tanks, jeeps, and trucks, but a second front was needed to take the pressure off the Soviet army.

In 1942 the Allies decided to invade the French territory of Northwest Africa. The invasion was called Operation Torch, and Eisenhower asked for Major General George Patton to be part of its command. Ike had great faith in his friend's ability to defeat the German commander, Erwin Rommel. But it was early in the war for U.S. soldiers, and they were not skilled at fighting. The GIs (U.S. soldiers) had trouble identifying enemy aircraft. They did not use their rifles and antiaircraft weapons accurately.

The Allies needed the suppport of the French, but that country's leadership was divided, making the Allied campaign more difficult. Some French people supported General Charles de Gaulle, leader of the French resistance movement, while

In Tunisia in March 1943, Ike discusses plans for Operation Torch with his friend George S. Patton. Ike chose Patton to help command the invasion of North Africa.

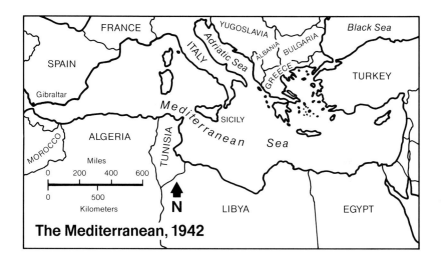

The Mediterranean, 1942

others favored Marshal Philippe Pétain, whose Vichy government collaborated with Germany.

Hoping to find a leader all French people could agree on, the Allies brought General Henri Giraud into North Africa. Unfortunately, French leaders in North Africa would not accept Giraud as their commander. They wanted Admiral of the Fleet Jean Darlan, a Vichy government member. Darlan hated the British and did not want to support the Allies. The Allies did not want to work with Darlan, either, because of his ties to Nazi Germany. Darlan was willing to work with the Allies if he could control French North Africa, however.

Eisenhower was a military leader rather than a politician, but he understood the danger involved in siding with Darlan. He knew his decision to accept Darlan as commander would be unpopular. Leaders all around the world would shout, "No! He cannot be trusted!" But Ike had to hurry. Time was running out. In return for Darlan's support, Ike authorized Darlan to handle French affairs in North Africa. This arrangement, which came to be known as the "Darlan Deal," was not very successful and stirred controversy in Britain and the U.S. It almost cost Eisenhower his command.

On November 4, 1942, Eisenhower ordered his pilot to ignore bad weather and head for Gibraltar, a peninsula on the coast of Spain. From there he commanded the Allied troops in North Africa. On November 8, 500 troop and supply ships and 350 warships carried Allied troops to the coast of Algeria and Morocco. Ike's friend Patton led the Western Tank Force ashore.

During one of the first battles, as Ike walked among his men, he came upon a soldier kneeling in the mud. The sight of the young man brought tears to his eyes. Blinking, he

President Roosevelt visited Ike in Sicily in December 1943 to tell him that he would be the one to command the invasion of France.

stood close so he could hear what the soldier was saying. "We pray for help that none of us may let a comrade down, that each of us may do his duty to himself, his comrades, and his country and—so be worthy of our American heritage."

The battle for North Africa took too long. Week after week, fighting raged. The Allies would take a hill, then lose it, then fight to take it again. It was Eisenhower's first command in battle. He was unsure of himself. He made mistakes, but he was determined to learn and determined to win.

In February 1943, Ike ordered a series of counterattacks which caused the Germans to fall back. He wished the engagement could have gone better, but Ike would have been pleased by what General Rommel wrote: "The American defense had been very skillfully executed."

By mid-May, the war in Africa was over. On May 10, 1943, Eisenhower's staff member Harry Butcher wrote in his diary, "Ike is nonchalant. For him the battle was finished some time ago; now his thoughts are on the next job against Hitler—Sicily."

Casualties in North Africa were heavy, but when the campaign was over, Ike's troops had won.

Soldiers prepare to land on the beaches of Normandy, France, on June 6, 1944 — the day that is known as "D-Day." The invasion, named Overlord, was a dramatic success.

∞ FIVE ∞

Operation Overlord

1944

*"It would be difficult to conceive of a more
soul-racking problem."*
—Dwight D. Eisenhower

By 1944, after successful Allied campaigns in Sicily and Italy, the time had come to make final plans for the Allied armies to push across the English Channel. The offensive would require thousands of men, landing craft, airplanes, and the cooperation of several governments. Eisenhower set up headquarters in London. From there he would command the operation, which was called Overlord.

As D-Day (the day of the operation) approached, anxieties rose. Officers were nervous. Heads of government quarreled. People were afraid, and the weather was so stormy that plans could not be firmly settled. In a letter to Mamie, Ike wrote, "I seem to live on a network of high tension wires." He could not tell her how close D-Day was because the date had to be kept secret. Ike worried that the Germans would learn of the Allies' plans.

Eisenhower points to the huge wall map at Supreme Headquarters of the Allied Expeditionary Force (SHAEF) in London. From here Ike planned and led the invasion of Normandy.

Sometimes Ike needed to get away from the pressures of war. He could escape and rest at Telegraph Cottage. Here Ike walked in the country with Telek. In the evening, he played cards with Kay Summersby, a secretary named Mary Alice Jaqua, and Harry Butcher.

But there were not many hours for relaxation. D-Day was set for June 5, 1944. And—there were problems. The Germans had more soldiers than the Allies. The Allies could not agree on how best to use airplanes. Some thought the bombers should be used to destroy French railroads so that the Germans could not travel easily through France. Others thought that German aircraft production factories and oil refineries should be bombed. There was also a worldwide shortage of landing craft. Worse than any of these was the worry of weather. Weather and tide conditions had to be just right for the invasion to go on. If it didn't take place on June 5 or 6, there would only be one other possible date.

It was raining on June 3 as Ike paced the floor. Were more storms coming? Sometimes the report was "yes"; other times, "no."

One report said, "It will rain on the 5th, but be clear on the 6th."

Another said, "It will rain on the 6th."

Still another predicted high winds.

Only Eisenhower, as supreme commander, could sort out the conflicting reports. Only the supreme commander could say, "The invasion is on." It was a lonely job.

That evening, Eisenhower met with his staff. RAF (Royal Air Force) Captain J. M. Stagg had bad news. "A high pressure system is moving out and a low pressure system is coming in. On June 5 the weather will be overcast and stormy. Clouds will be down on the ground. There will be strong winds."

If the invasion was going to be on, the navy's big ships would have to start toward England. If D-Day was postponed, however, they would have to stay far out at sea. Finally Eisenhower sent a message to his aide, "Start your voyage, but due to weather, there may be a last-minute cancellation."

At 4:30 the next morning, Sunday, June 4, Eisenhower met with his staff. Stagg said that conditions at sea would be better than anticipated, but fog would be thick. British

General Bernard Montgomery wanted to go ahead anyway. Air Marshal Arthur Tedder wanted to wait. Admiral Bertram Ramsay, the naval commander, said the navy would do its part, but he remained neutral. Eisenhower remarked that Overlord would succeed only because of Allied air superiority. The officers thought about it and finally agreed. Overlord was postponed for 24 hours, to June 6. Secret orders were sent to the navy. The commanders slowed their ships.

That evening the wind blew and the rain pelted against the windows at headquarters. Officers lounged in easy chairs and stared at a big map on the wall. Would they be going the day after tomorrow? Would they follow the lines that curved and twisted on the map, showing the invasion? Coffee was served, and conversation moved from subject to subject. One minute they talked about the war, and the next, they tried to forget. At 9:30 P.M., Stagg came in with the latest weather report.

"Good news! We're getting a break! The weather will clear!"

Excitement exploded through the building. The officers could hardly stop cheering.

Stagg said the rain would let up in about three hours, and there would be 36 hours of clear weather. Bombers would be able to fly on Monday night.

But 36 hours was not very long. Could the troops make it across the Channel? Could they fight their way up from the beaches and drive far enough inland before another storm hit? What if the bombers were grounded? The invasion would be risky. The responsibility weighed heavily on Eisenhower. He was tempted to postpone Overlord again.

Admiral Ramsay told him that the fleet "must be told in the next half hour if Overlord is to take place on Tuesday. . . a further postponement would be forty-eight hours."

The silence was heavy. Then Brigadier General Walter Bedell Smith said, "It's a gamble but it's the best possible gamble."

Eisenhower nodded, paced, then asked General Montgomery, "Do you see any reason for not going Tuesday?"

Montgomery looked Eisenhower in the eye. "I would say—go!"

Eisenhower turned and paced some more. Finally he stopped walking, looked around at his commanders, and said, "The question is, just how long can you hang this operation on the end of a limb and let it hang there?"

It seemed impossible that the rain would stop, but early the next morning, the supreme commander gave the order, "O.K., let's go." Once again excited cheers rang through headquarters.

The commanders rushed outside and headed for their posts. The room fell silent. Everyone was gone—everyone but Eisenhower. D-Day had begun and he was alone. The officers leading their troops would play a more active role during the invasion than Eisenhower. Eisenhower, the supreme commander, could only wait.

But Ike was getting better at killing time. He visited the South Parade Pier in Portsmouth to see the British soldiers climb aboard their landing craft. He played a game of checkers with Butcher. He scrawled a press release to be used if D-Day failed. It said, "Our landings... have failed... and I have withdrawn troops. If fault or blame attaches to the attempt it is mine alone."

At 6:00 P.M., he and his driver went to Newbury to watch the 101st Airborne Division prepare for their flight to Normandy. Eisenhower wandered among the men. Their faces were blackened, and their packs, guns, and personal equipment were scattered on the ground. When they recognized Ike, groups of soldiers gathered around him.

"Don't worry," Ike said. "You have the best equipment and the best leaders."

A sergeant told him, "We ain't worried, General. It's the Krauts that ought to be worrying now."

A private shouted, "Look out, Hitler, here we come."

A Texan promised Eisenhower a job on his cattle ranch.

When the last plane rumbled into the sky, Ike turned to Kay. There were tears in his eyes. "Well," he said quietly, "it's on."

Throughout the next morning, news from the beachhead

Troopers wade ashore to the beaches of Normandy. The invasion took the Germans by surprise and marked an important victory for the Allies.

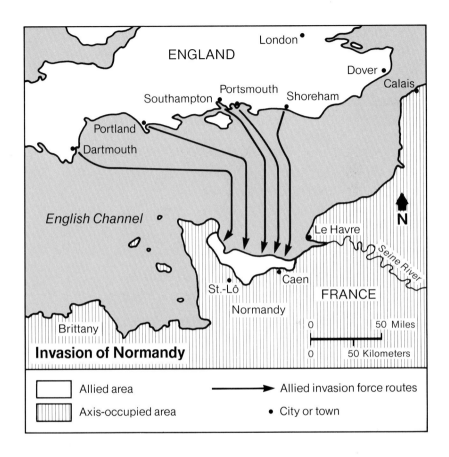

Invasion of Normandy

Allied area

Axis-occupied area

Allied invasion force routes

• City or town

was spotty, but it was clear that the Germans had been fooled. Eisenhower sent a message to Marshall informing him that the battle seemed to be going well. He told him that he had seen the troops and "the light of battle was in their eyes."

The hours slowly ticked away as Eisenhower paced, his mood changing back and forth from joy to worry. By nightfall the Allies were victorious. More than 23,000 airborne troops had been dropped into Normandy, and 57,000 U.S. and 75,000 British and Canadian troops had reached the beaches of France.

On June 7, 1944, Eisenhower boarded the British

minelayer *Apollo* and visited the Normandy beachhead. Lieutenant General Omar Bradley came aboard to tell Ike of the situation.

"It's generally good," he said. "The troops have moved off the beaches and are driving inland."

The Germans were fighting hard, but they could not move in reinforcements fast enough. Bombers had destroyed the railroads and blown apart bridges.

Eisenhower's gamble on the weather had paid off. What Winston Churchill, prime minister of England, called "the most difficult and complicated operation that has ever taken place" had put the Allies back on the continent of Europe.

Ike became a hero.

∽ SIX ∾

The Road to Victory

1944-1945

*"It's all so terrible, so awful, that I constantly
wonder how 'civilization' can stand war at all."*
—Dwight D. Eisenhower

By August 23, 1944, after two and a half months of bitter fighting, to some people the end of the war seemed near. Intelligence officers in London said of the German army, "No recovery is now possible." Patton believed he could cross the German border in 10 days. The First Army liberated Paris. The 21st Army swept across Europe, covering 200 miles. Romania and Finland surrendered to the Soviet Union, and the Germans pulled out of Greece. But Ike viewed the war differently. He did not see it as almost finished. The general was right—the Germans dug in.

The war dragged on. Montgomery disagreed with Ike's strategies. Heads of governments argued about how the war should be fought. The Germans were tough. They were fighting for their lives. They would not give up.

On December 16, in his headquarters at Versailles,

France, Ike threw a party to celebrate three events: Ike's receiving his fifth star and promotion to general of the army; the marriage of Mickey McKeogh (a soldier who had been with Ike for five years) to a WAC (Women's Army Corps) member; and Kay Summersby's receiving the British Empire Medal. Ike now enjoyed the same rank as Marshall, MacArthur, and Montgomery.

The morning was filled with fun and laughter, but the afternoon brought bad news. British General Kenneth Strong told them that the Germans had launched an attack in the forest of the Ardennes, a hilly region in southern Belgium. A hush fell over the room, then Strong continued, "We need more men. We need to replace the soldiers we've lost."

Suddenly faces were glum, lips turned down, and brows pushed together. The officers began to pace and argue. One said the attack was not serious—Strong was exaggerating. Another said the drive was serious, but it would soon lessen.

Eisenhower didn't think the Germans would stop. "We must send more troops." He argued that they should take troops from Patton.

Before the Allied armies could move forward, they had to face a last-stand German onslaught in the Ardennes forest. Hitler had chosen this hilly, wooded region to strike suddenly. He and his advisers had found the Allies' weakest point, and the Germans quickly overran the U.S. Army. The GIs were helpless as German tanks rumbled forward. Officers in command were surprised, shocked, and depressed. Eisenhower called a conference on December 19 to plan a counterattack.

Generals George Patton, Jacob Devers, and Omar Bradley

Ike chats with a soldier in Belgium in 1944.

hovered near a potbellied stove in a cold, damp squad room. They were worried about the war and embarrassed by mistakes they had made. Realizing how his officers felt, Ike opened the meeting by saying, "The present situation is to be regarded as one of opportunity for us and not of disaster. There will be only cheerful faces at this conference table."

Ike ordered the Services of Supply to release all men who were able to fight. He ordered service units to guard the bridges across the Meuse River. In case of retreat, he emphasized, no bridge must fall into enemy hands. Adding to the panic, the Germans had organized a special group of soldiers who spoke English and dressed in American uniforms. They were given captured American jeeps to drive behind the Allies' lines. Their mission was to issue false orders and to kill the supreme commander.

Area of Maximum Axis Rule in Europe, 1941-42

North Sea

NORWAY

GREAT BRITAIN

IRELAND

DENMARK

ENGLAND

NETHERLANDS

London

English Channel

Berlin

Atlantic

Ocean

Antwerp

BELGIUM

GERMANY

Invasion of Normandy

Bastogne

Paris

Battle of the Bulge

LUX.

Rhine River

CZE

FRANCE

SWITZERLAND

AUSTRIA*

SPAIN

PORTUGAL

ITALY

Gibraltar

Mediterranean Sea

SICILY

Invasion of Sicily

*In March 1938, German soldiers marched into Austria and united it with Germany.

Security was tightened. Ike was guarded day and night. He could not walk outside headquarters unless he was surrounded by soldiers carrying guns. When he traveled into the country, he was protected by military police in jeeps.

One day Ike could no longer stand the confinement. "I'm going out for a walk," he said as he slipped out the back door of headquarters. "If anyone wants to shoot me, he can go right ahead."

The battle raged on in the Ardennes forest. Skies were overcast and airplanes could not fly. "Weather," Eisenhower mumbled between his teeth. "Our greatest enemy is weather." He hoped the Germans wouldn't take advantage of the overcast sky.

But the Germans were quick to move under the blanket of fog. Their tanks rumbled westward and overran the Allies. German engines roared as they ground their way in and out of ravines. The iron monsters sloshed through mud and knocked down trees. The infantry was close behind. The fog was still hanging low when the Germans wheeled to the right toward the port of Antwerp. It was the beginning of a famous battle, which the Allies called the Battle of the Bulge and the Germans, Operation Watch on the Rhine.

Eisenhower remained calm. With a cool head, he studied the military threat. The British historian Arthur Bryant wrote, "Calamity acted on Eisenhower like a restorative and brought out all the greatness in his character."

On December 22, with headquarters wrapped in fog, the supreme commander issued an Order of the Day: "We cannot be content with [the Germans'] mere repulse. By rushing out from his fixed defenses the enemy may give us the chance to turn his great gamble into his worst defeat. . . . Let everyone hold before him a single thought—to destroy the enemy on the ground, in the air, everywhere—destroy him!"

That morning the Germans stopped fighting long enough to ask U.S. Brigadier General Anthony McAuliffe for the Allies' surrender. "Nuts," said the general. His answer to the Germans became famous.

Americans soldiers were saying, "The Germans stuck their neck out—that's the best thing that could have happened."

On December 23, there was good news. The sun broke through the clouds and the sky turned blue. Cheers were heard all around headquarters. Pilots rolled off beds and jumped up from chairs. They ran to their fighter planes and revved up the engines. C-47 airplanes lumbered into the air and headed cross-country to drop supplies. With air cover, Patton fired up his tanks and began his drive to the city of Bastogne, Belgium. Montgomery sent a message to Eisenhower: "The First Army is in good trim."

Even though the sun was shining, the days were difficult for Ike. The French leaders quarreled. Montgomery was slow to move his troops. Mamie was upset because Ike didn't write. John had graduated from West Point and had received orders to leave for Europe. And the weather was bitter cold. The Germans were used to fighting in snow. The Allies were not.

With a heavy heart, Ike wrote a hurried note to his wife. "War is truly a brutal business!" He knew Mamie worried about John being in a war zone, and wrote, "We must be of good courage—we must hang on to faith and hope—and we must believe in the ultimate purposes of a merciful God."

About the war, he said, "We are hammering away.

While his father was fighting the war in Europe, John Eisenhower graduated from the Military Academy at West Point. Mamie worried that John would be sent abroad to fight.

Regardless of setbacks, disappointments, and everything else, we are on the road to victory! What a boon peace will be to this poor old world!" In another letter, he added, "If ever I have to be in another war I'm going to take you along!"

Eisenhower had been correct when he told Mamie that victory in the "Bulge" was near. But when the Germans surrendered in that battle in February 1945, the news that followed divided the Allies and caused a terrible uproar.

Montgomery held a news conference and told reporters that it was the English who won the Battle of the Bulge. Then he said something the Americans could not forgive. "The GIs make great fighting men when given the proper leadership."

The U.S. generals were furious. Patton ranted and raved to every reporter who would listen. He told them that the Americans had the battle won before Montgomery came in. Bradley was angry as well.

In fact, Montgomery had not been the victorious general.

Instead, he had gotten in everyone's way and made the counterattack difficult. Patton wrote in his diary, "Had it not been for Montgomery, we could have bagged the whole German army."

With the Battle of the Bulge behind them, the "Big Three" (the Soviet Union, England, and the United States) argued. They wanted to end the war. But how? Which way should they go? Who would do this? Who would do that? They could not agree.

When the Soviets began their winter offensive into Germany, Eisenhower commented, "I hope [they] keep right on going into the heart of Germany." But Churchill viewed

Ike talks with Winston Churchill.

the Soviets as "a mortal danger to the free world." "They must not get to Berlin first," he said. "Berlin is important!"

U.S. leaders had not established a policy about that important city. Although the decision was controversial, the Allies decided that the Soviets would enter Berlin. Once again, "the smell of victory was in the air."

Airplanes flew, tanks rumbled, and infantrymen sloshed their way over rough terrain. From all directions, the Allied armies closed in on the Germans. Canadian troops liberated the Netherlands. The British Second Army headed north. Bradley's group raced eastward. In the south, Allied armies pushed toward Czechoslovakia.

German troopers surrender to U.S. soldiers of the 100th Infantry in Italy in 1944. German armies were retreating everywhere, and Allied victory in World War II was close at hand.

Hitler's military adviser Alfred Jodl signs Germany's surrender papers in Reims, France, in 1945, marking the end of the war in Europe.

While the Allied forces rolled toward victory in Europe, back in the U.S., President Roosevelt's health was failing. He died on April 12, 1945. Harry S Truman became the 33d president of the United States.

Changes were also occurring in Germany. Heinrich Himmler, head of the Nazi secret police, tried to surrender to Great Britain and the United States. But the Allies demanded that German troops surrender on all fronts—they must surrender to the Soviet Union on the east as well. On April 30, Hitler and his wife committed suicide.

Early in the morning on May 7, 1945, Germany surrendered. It had been five years, eight months, and six days since World War II had started. With the Germans' defeat, the war in Europe had ended. The supreme commander dictated a message to Chief of Staff Marshall. It read, "The mission of this Allied force was fulfilled at 0241 local time, May 7, 1945."

George C. Marshall sent a reply back to Eisenhower. "You have completed your mission with the greatest victory in the history of warfare...." he said. "You have made history, great history for the good of mankind and you have stood for all we hope for and admire in an officer of the United States Army."

⧉ SEVEN ⧉

A Hero Comes Home

1945-1951

*"General, there is nothing that you may want that
I won't try to help you get. That definitely and
specifically includes the presidency in 1948."*
—Harry S Truman, speaking to Eisenhower

The war in Europe was over! Radio commentators interrupted programs to tell the news. "Germany has surrendered!" Cablegrams reached across the ocean. "They've laid down their arms!" Telegrams read, "Hurrah! Hurrah!" Telephone booths were filled with excited young men calling their girlfriends: "I can hardly wait to see you."

Back home in the U.S., horns blew and whistles shrieked. Confetti streamed down from high windows. Mothers began to plan for their sons' return and wives waited anxiously by telephones. Across the ocean, soldiers were eager to tear off their uniforms. They wanted to go back to their old jobs or back to school.

Eisenhower was not unlike the young soldiers. He told Mamie he'd come home as soon as he could. There was much work to be done, but there was time to celebrate.

On May 15, Ike spent the night in London. His son John, Kay Summersby, Omar Bradley, and British aide Jimmy Gault accompanied him. They visited Telegraph Cottage, ate dinner, and went to the theater.

When the people in the audience spotted Ike, they shouted, "Speech! Speech!" From his box in the balcony, Ike stood and said, "It's nice to be back in a country where I can *almost* speak the language." The theater thundered with applause. Ike was surprised to discover how famous he had become.

Churchill asked Ike to take part in a celebration at Guildhall, a large public meeting hall in London. Eisenhower was nervous when he walked to the podium to speak, but his words were grand. "I come from the very heart of America," he said. He spoke of the differences between Abilene and London, then told how they were alike. "To preserve his freedom of worship, his equality before the law, his liberty to speak and act as he sees fit . . . a Londoner will fight. So will a citizen of Abilene. When we consider these things, then the valley of the Thames [a river in England] draws closer to the farms of Kansas."

In June Ike was ready to return to the U.S. He and John boarded a plane for New York. Ike fastened his seat belt, leaned back, and looked at his son. "Well," he said, "now I've got to figure out what I'm going to say when I get there."

When they arrived, there were 2,000,000 people waiting to greet the general—the man who had won the war in Europe. Ike wove his way through the crowd, then stood on the steps of City Hall. Still not believing his popularity, he said, "I'm just a Kansas farmer boy who did his duty."

Mamie had hoped to spend some quiet time with Ike, but she had to share him with the public. It seemed that

The victorious supreme commander waves to the crowd gathered in New York City in June 1945 to celebrate his return.

every organization in the U.S. wanted him to speak. Wherever he went, people loved him. His words, "Oh, God, it's swell to be back!" made headlines in the Washington, D.C., paper. The city of New York held a parade in his honor. Once again whistles blew and confetti drifted down from buildings. Ike rode slowly past the cheering crowds in an open convertible. He waved and grinned. People on the sidewalks nudged each other saying, "Isn't he handsome?—He waved at me—He's wonderful, just wonderful."

All over the United States, people began to say, "Ike should be president." But when a friend wrote and asked him how it felt to be a presidential candidate, Ike grabbed a pencil and scribbled, "Baloney! Why can't a simple soldier be left alone to carry out his orders? And I furiously object to the word 'candidate'—I ain't and won't."

Ike was tired. He had fulfilled his duty to his country. He wanted to retire to a farm and be with Mamie. But it was not easy for such a popular man to slip away. President Truman wanted Eisenhower to head the U.S. occupation zone in Germany. Eisenhower felt it was his duty, so he went back to Europe.

Ike wanted to bring Mamie with him, but Truman would not allow it. Once again the Eisenhowers were separated. It was a lonely period in Ike's life. His only joy was John, who was stationed nearby. John later wrote that these months were "probably the period in my entire life when Dad and I were closest."

On May 25, 1945, Eisenhower moved his headquarters to Frankfurt, Germany. He told Butcher that "the job of fighting the war was not so wearing" as the job of running the occupation.

He followed his orders by forbidding Allied soldiers to

be friendly with the Germans. He called for automatic arrest of Germans who belonged to Nazi organizations. He removed Nazis from public office. His instructions said that it was his responsibility to make the Germans realize that their suffering was their own fault. Eisenhower believed in what he was doing. He hated the Germans because they had killed millions of innocent Jews. He hated them because of their brutal warfare. In letters to Mamie he wrote, "The German is a beast," and "God, I hate the Germans!"

The United States was still at war with Japan. It was Secretary of War Henry L. Stimson who first told Eisenhower about the atomic bomb, a new, powerful weapon. When Ike learned of the bomb's ability to kill, he was depressed. He felt that Japan was already defeated and that "dropping the bomb was completely unnecessary."

Stimson was upset by Eisenhower's attitude. He argued that using the bomb would end the war. Eisenhower disagreed. He thought that using such a weapon would shock the world.

Three days later, Eisenhower flew to Berlin to meet President Truman. "Don't use the bomb," he told Truman. He said that the Japanese were already defeated, and the fighting would soon end. Ike pleaded, but no one listened.

On August 6, 1945, a B-29 called *Enola Gay* dropped an atomic bomb on the city of Hiroshima. Three days later, a second bomb was dropped on the city of Nagasaki. On September 2, aboard the battleship *Missouri* in Tokyo Bay, the Japanese surrendered. General MacArthur signed for the Allies. It was the end of World War II.

Eisenhower left Europe on November 11, 1945, to live in

Eisenhower strongly opposed the use of the atomic bomb against Japan, but Truman authorized it anyway. Shown here is the explosion of the bomb dropped on Hiroshima.

Washington and become chief of staff of the U.S. Army. He still dreamed of retiring to a farm, but once again that wish was set aside. He did not care for his new position, but he was back home and Mamie was with him.

Now Eisenhower faced a different kind of battle. His war was with other generals. They fought over military training for all citizens. He battled with Congress over the size of a postwar army. In a letter to John he wrote, "The Pentagon was a sorry place to light after having commanded a theater of war."

Eisenhower called for a strong army. He never wanted to see another war—never wanted to hear another gun fired. He felt the only way to ensure peace was to keep the army strong.

When he spoke at Boston University in 1946, he asked educators to "teach people to put the people of my profession out of a job." He urged that students be taught that understanding is worthwhile—that differences are not so great they can't be solved.

On June 10, 1947, John Eisenhower married Barbara Thompson in the chapel at Fort Monroe, Virginia. Ike was delighted to have a daughter in the family, but his life was mostly taken up by outside pressures. More often now individuals and organizations were asking him to run for the office of president in 1948. He had no desire to be president, but no one believed him. Once a reporter asked, "Now, General, isn't there some circumstance, some very remote circumstance, that might induce you to get into politics?"

Eisenhower turned on his heel to face the man. "Look, son," he said. "I cannot conceive of any circumstance that could drag out of me permission to consider me for any political post from dogcatcher to Grand High Supreme King of the Universe!"

Although most people did not consider Eisenhower an academic, he served as president of Columbia University from 1948 to 1953.

On October 14, 1947, Eisenhower was 57 years old. His term as chief of staff was finished. Offers of employment came from many major corporations. He finally accepted a position as president of Columbia University. He took office in June 1948.

During Ike's years at Columbia, the Eisenhowers became grandparents. Dwight David II was born in 1948, and 14 months later, Barbara Anne. A third grandchild, Susan Elaine, was born in 1951. Ike also found time to paint, and he quit smoking. He wrote his war memoirs, called *Crusade in Europe*, which were published in late 1948. He met a group of wealthy, powerful men whom he began calling "the gang." Eisenhower was their hero. They began to tell Ike that the American people needed him to be their president.

✺ EIGHT ✺

Crusade for the Presidency

1950-1952

"I accept your summons. I will lead this crusade."
—Dwight D. Eisenhower

On June 25, 1950, the peace that the Allied nations had struggled for came to an end. It happened when the Communist North Koreans marched over the 38th parallel (which separated North and South Korea) into non-Communist South Korea.

This invasion angered members of the United Nations. They said that the North Koreans had violated international peace terms. President Truman called on the U.S. to help and not to let the Communists take over South Korea. He sent the U.S. Navy and the Air Force. He promised ground troops.

The invasion of South Korea caused concern among countries of Western Europe that had signed the North Atlantic Treaty. The group was called NATO (North Atlantic Treaty Organization) and provided common defense against aggressive nations.

Heads of government on both sides of the Atlantic Ocean were saying, "We want Eisenhower to command NATO." Truman asked Eisenhower to accept the position.

Ike was pleased. "I am a soldier," he said, "and am ready to respond to whatever orders my superiors...may care to issue to me." It was an ideal appointment for Ike. He was happy to take a leave of absence from Columbia. Eisenhower told his son, "I consider this to be the most important military job in the world." NATO headquarters were in Paris, so Ike and Mamie moved there.

While Ike served as commander of NATO, his friends were telling him that he was the "only man" who could lead the U.S. "You must be president," they said. Ike was slowly beginning to agree with them when Jacqueline Cochran, a famous aviator, flew to Paris. She brought with her a two-hour film of an Eisenhower rally that 15,000 people had attended. The film showed the crowd waving "I Like Ike" banners while chanting "We want Ike!"

Mamie and Ike were moved by the film. After it was over, Cochran raised her glass to Eisenhower and blurted, "To the president!" Feelings of love, patriotism, and duty moved within Ike. The Kansas farm boy, the general, and the supreme commander all lived within this man. With tears in his eyes, he said the words that thousands of Americans had been waiting to hear: "I'm going to run."

Ike began to plan his campaign. He had been a reluctant candidate, but if he was going to be in the race, he was in it to win. In April 1952, he issued his final NATO report and asked to go home. He no longer wished to lead NATO; he had decided to become a candidate for the Republican nomination.

Back home, his supporters bombarded him with advice. "Don't say this," they said; "don't do that." He found himself skirting the issues and dodging questions. He felt depressed. He didn't like being in a position in which he couldn't speak his mind.

But there were compensations. One reward came in a letter from British Field Marshal Alan Brooke. It said, "Personally I thank God that you have decided [to run for president] for I feel that the future security of the world depends on your now assuming this great office."

Rumors began to fly. "Mamie has a drinking problem." "Kay Summersby and Eisenhower are in love." The rumors were started by the opposing political party. None of them were true. Truman told Ike, "If that's all it is, Ike, then you can just figure you're lucky." Ike had been afraid he was going to hate the whole business of running for president. Now he was sure of it. But he was in the race and he was determined to win. "Having put my hand to the plow," he said, "I intend to see the job through to the end of the furrow."

His first task was to gain more Republican delegates than his opponent before the Republican convention. The Republican who won the most delegates would then run against the most popular Democratic candidate. His opponent, Robert Taft, was well known and wanted to be president.

On June 4, 1952, at Abilene, he gave his first televised political speech. He said that he was against inflation, heavy taxation, too much government, dishonesty, and corruption. He was for civil rights and a free marketplace. He said that if there were any Communists in government, they would be ousted. His speech won him delegates, but it made Ike uneasy. "Everything is calculated; the natural and the spontaneous are frowned upon severely," he wrote.

In June 1952, at Abilene, Eisenhower gave his first political speech. Eisenhower didn't like having to choose his words so carefully, but reporters appreciated his "natural warmth."

That was how Eisenhower felt. Other people had different opinions. Some said he answered the reporters' questions as well as President Roosevelt had. Some said he answered them better. One commentator concluded, "He is direct."

On June 26, he addressed a crowd of 11,000 admirers in the Denver Coliseum and a national television and radio audience. Movie stars warmed up the crowd before he began. Ike said what the Republicans wanted to hear: "If we had been less soft and weak, there would probably have been no war in Korea!" He promised to make the United States strong by handling the national budget in a responsible manner. "A bankrupt America," he said, "is a defenseless America."

"I'm going to win," he told Mamie the next morning as they rode the train into Taft country, the Great Plains. Here he met with politicians and gave speeches. Many people feared Communism and the Soviet Union. Ike tried to calm their fears. He told audiences he did not like the way politicians stirred up "scary talk" about Russia. He said he didn't think that "every Russian is fourteen feet high." He said that if the American people would pull together, there was no more reason to fear the Russians "than there is to fear pollywogs swimming down a muddy creek."

On July 5, Eisenhower set up headquarters in Chicago, where the Republican national convention was to be held. He met with delegates and governors. But he was not used to political maneuvering. He was uncomfortable as the politicians zeroed in on the final hour. "Stay in your room," his managers told him. "We'll take care of last-minute arrangements." Ike was happy to take their advice.

After months of hard work, sleepless nights, and anxious moments, the convention was held. Speeches were made. Flags waved, and the audience applauded thunderously. Taft was nominated by Senator Everett Dirksen of Illinois. Governor Theodore McKeldin of Maryland nominated Eisenhower. At the end of the first round of voting, Eisenhower had 595 votes, 9 short of victory. Then the delegation from Minnesota shifted its votes to Eisenhower. This made Ike the winner. "It's Ike!" someone shouted. "Ike's won!" The band played. Balloons floated toward the ceiling. Men and women marched with banners. Eisenhower was the Republican nominee for the presidency in 1952. California senator Richard Nixon became his running mate. If Eisenhower won against the Democrats, Nixon would be vice president.

On July 14, the Eisenhowers flew to Denver to set

Ike emerged the winner at the Republican convention.

up headquarters in the Brown Palace Hotel. From here Ike selected his staff and planned his campaign. He was to run against Adlai Stevenson, the Democratic governor from Illinois.

Eisenhower decided to go on a "whistle-stop" campaign, traveling by railroad all across the country. The train was nicknamed "Look Ahead, Neighbor." It rumbled from state to state, stopping in many towns. Crowds came waving "We Like Ike" banners. High school bands played while Ike and Mamie stood on the train's platform. When his audience was quiet, Ike gave a speech. "We need your support," he said. "Join our crusade." The crowds cheered. Then the train's whistle blew and it was time to move on. Ike and Mamie waved as "Look Ahead, Neighbor" whistled and tooted on down the track. In the eight-week campaign, the Eisenhowers

Crowds gathered in hundreds of small towns to see the popular candidate and his wife speak from the back of the "Look Ahead, Neighbor" train during Ike's whistle-stop campaign.

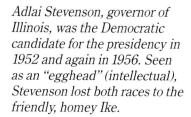

Adlai Stevenson, governor of Illinois, was the Democratic candidate for the presidency in 1952 and again in 1956. Seen as an "egghead" (intellectual), Stevenson lost both races to the friendly, homey Ike.

traveled over 50,000 miles through 45 states. Ike spoke in 232 towns.

Americans thought Mamie looked "smashing." Her bangs became an overnight fad. People liked the Eisenhower's "folksy" ways. In North Carolina, a crowd gathered around their train at 5:30 A.M. The general and his wife crawled out of bed and put on their bathrobes. Still half-asleep, they groped their way to the rear of the train. When the sleepy couple stepped out on the platform, the people cheered and laughed. How they loved this courageous couple!

But soon the campaign ran into trouble. Richard Nixon was accused of having "secret funds" and accepting gifts. "He bought a mink coat with campaign money," his opponents said.

Nixon overreacted. He said the story was a smear by the Communists. An article in the Republican *Herald Tribune* asked Nixon to withdraw from the race. Panic spread among the Republicans, but Eisenhower remained cool. Ike thought back to the problems he had encountered when he worked with leaders during the war. He remembered differences he'd had with Montgomery and Churchill. He called on his experience with handling people and decided to address the public.

In a television broadcast, he said: "I have long admired and applauded Senator Nixon's American faith and the determination to drive Communist sympathizers from offices of public trust. There has recently been leveled against him a charge of unethical practices. I believe Dick Nixon to be an honest man. I am confident that he will place all the facts before the American people fairly and squarely."

Nixon refused. Pressure grew for Ike to remove him from the ticket. Eisenhower was angry. Reluctantly he telephoned his running mate. He said, "I don't want to be in the position of condemning an innocent man. I think you ought to go on a nationwide television program and tell them

Richard Nixon served as vice president for two terms during Eisenhower's administration. Nixon later went on to become president in 1968. He was re-elected in 1972. In 1974, Nixon became the only president ever to resign from office.

Eisenhower's catchy campaign slogan was "I Like Ike." U.S. citizens showed that they did indeed like Ike when they voted him president on November 8, 1952.

everything there is to tell, everything you can remember since the day you entered public life."

Nixon asked if an announcement could be made after the program—one way or the other. Was he going to be the vice presidential candidate or not?

Eisenhower was thinking of what Nixon might say when he answered, "We will wait three or four days after the television show to see what the effect of the program is."

Nixon was angry, but this time Nixon took Ike's suggestion. What he said made history and is known as the "Checkers speech." It was so clever that it saved his position. He said that he had not used any of the campaign money for himself. His wife wore not a fur coat, but a "respectable Republican cloth coat." He said he had accepted only one personal gift, a cocker spaniel named Checkers.

Nixon also demanded that the Democratic candidates tell where their money came from and how much money they had. With that statement, he had put Eisenhower on the spot, too, because now Ike would have to do the same. He was so mad, he jammed his pencil into the paper where he

Mamie Eisenhower traveled with Ike all over the country during the campaign. Mamie's popularity helped win votes for her husband.

had been taking notes. Nixon stayed on the ticket, but Ike never trusted him again.

The people continued to like Ike. The high point of his campaign came in Detroit on October 24, when he promised that he would go to Korea to see what he could do about ending the war.

On election day, Ike and Mamie took the train to New York, where they cast their ballots. Early returns showed a massive switch of Democrats to the Republican party. Eisenhower was getting 55 percent of the popular vote. When the final count was in, Eisenhower had 33,936,234 votes. Stevenson had 27,314,992.

Eisenhower had won. Soon he would be the most powerful man in the world.

Harry S Truman congratulated Eisenhower as he was sworn in
as 34th president of the United States on January 20, 1953. Ike's
experiences in the army had helped prepare him for his new duties.

❧ NINE ❧

The First Term

1952-1957

*"I believe frantically in the American form
of democracy."*
—Dwight D. Eisenhower

Eisenhower kept his campaign promise and flew to Korea on November 29, 1952. John met him, along with Generals Mark Clark and James Van Fleet. "Welcome to the Land of the Morning Calm!" they said. It didn't seem very calm to Ike. Big guns could be heard in the distance, and Ike could see the mouths of caves where the North Koreans hid their cannons. It was winter and bitter cold. Ike and the generals walked through snow to visit combat units and talk with senior commanders. Bundled in a heavy, fur-lined jacket and thick boots, Ike visited the 15th Infantry. He stood in a "chow line" with GIs, then sat on an ammunition box to eat pork chops. He met Syngman Rhee, president of South Korea. He visited the city of Seoul, where refugees from North Korea huddled in flimsy shacks.

On January 20, 1953, Dwight Eisenhower became the

34th president of the United States. When he stepped up to the podium to give his Inaugural Address, he looked serious. Then his grim expression gave way to his famous grin. His arms shot up over his head in a V-for-Victory sign. The crowd cheered. When it was quiet again, Ike read his prayer: "Almighty God...make full and complete our dedication to the service of the people in this throng, and their fellow citizens everywhere."

Ike paused, then delivered his speech. He said the country's challenges were twofold: the dangers of war and of Communism. He promised that he would never stop seeking an honorable, worldwide peace, and that faith would unite all free people. He spoke of freedom, exclaiming that "a soldier's pack is not so heavy a burden as a prisoner's chains."

After his first day as president, Ike wrote in his diary, "[Today seems] like a continuation of all I've been doing since July 1941."

But some of his responsibilities were different. Instead of managing troops, now he struggled with the "cold war," foreign trade, low-cost housing, slum clearance, and better Social Security for seniors. Senator Joseph McCarthy caused many problems while he searched for Communists in government, and every day Ike asked himself, "What should we do about the atom bomb? Should we keep the bomb for ourselves, or share it with friendly countries?"

While Ike was busy running the country, Mamie was busy running the White House. She managed a housekeeping staff that took care of 132 rooms. She helped her husband entertain 26 kings. Prime ministers and other heads of state came from all over the world.

Ike was ready for the task. He was 62 years old and in good health. He exercised regularly, ate and drank in

*One presidential duty is to entertain foreign leaders. Here,
the Eisenhowers host a visit by England's Queen Elizabeth and
Prince Philip.*

moderation, and he had stopped smoking. He was an
experienced leader. His friend Bernard Law Montgomery
said of Eisenhower, "He has the power of drawing the hearts
of men towards him as a magnet attracts the bits of metal.
He merely has to smile at you, and you trust him at once."

The presidency was difficult, but Eisenhower had learned
valuable lessons as supreme commander. One of the most
important was teamwork. "I don't believe this government,"
he said, "was set up to be operated by anyone acting alone."

Joseph Stalin died on March 5, 1953. With the passing of its dictator, Eisenhower hoped the Soviet Union would be more friendly. He hoped that now the two countries could work together toward peace and end the cold war. In April he gave a famous speech called "The Chance for Peace."

Ike said, "The cost of one modern heavy bomber is this: a modern brick school in more than thirty cities.... It is two fine, fully equipped hospitals. We pay for a single fighter plane with a half-million bushels of wheat. We pay for a single destroyer with new homes that could have housed more than eight thousand people.

"This is not a way of life at all, in any true sense. Under the cloud of threatening war, it is humanity hanging from a cross of iron."

The president said that if the Soviet Union was ready for peace, the U.S. would devote part of the savings achieved by disarmament for world aid. With this speech, Ike had established the United States' leadership in the world.

He was leading in all ways. The Korean War ended and an armistice was signed on July 26, 1953. Acclaim for Eisenhower poured in from around the world.

Life in the White House was hectic, but Ike was accustomed to long hours and hard work. At 6:00 A.M. each day, he slipped out of bed, trying not to waken Mamie. Two or three suits had been laid out for him in his dressing room. (Most of his clothes were custom-made and given to him by a New York clothes manufacturer.) He selected the suit he wished to wear and dressed for the day. He read the morning papers over breakfast, then went to his office at 8:00 A.M. The noon meal was usually combined with work, but sometimes after lunch he played a round of golf on the White House lawn. On those days, he went back to his office until 6:00 P.M. If no conferences were scheduled after dinner, he read reports or painted.

In the months that followed, Ike's responsibilities grew. Blacks in the South fought for civil rights, and the Supreme Court ruled to integrate schools. Important decisions had to be made concerning the arms race and the use of the atomic bomb. The spread of Communism was a threat, and the cold war posed a national problem. Senator Joseph McCarthy of Wisconsin blasted forth about the conspiracy of Communists he claimed to have uncovered in Washington.

Eisenhower consults with John Foster Dulles, secretary of state. Dulles fought strenuously against Communism in the world.

Eisenhower tried to spend time with his family in the White House. From left: David, Mamie, Barbara, Mary, John, Anne, Dwight, and Susan.

In September of 1955, Eisenhower had his first bout with poor health. The Eisenhowers had gone to a ranch at Fraser, Colorado. On the morning of the 23d, Ike was up at 5:00 A.M. After breakfast, he and his friend George Allen drove to Cherry Hills Golf Course in Denver, where Ike planned to relax and have a good time. But twice he was called to the clubhouse for phone calls. He scored badly, his stomach hurt from his lunch of hamburgers and onions, and his temper was flaring. During the evening, he shot billiards with a friend, then went to bed at 10:00 P.M. At 1:30 A.M., he awoke with a pain in his chest. A terrible pain!

Mamie was frightened. "I'll call the doctor," she said.

Dr. Howard Snyder came in a hurry. He put medicine under Ike's tongue and gave him shots. "Stay in bed," he said, "and keep warm."

In the morning, Ike was transferred to the hospital. The president of the United States had suffered a heart attack.

By the end of the second day after the attack, Ike was planning on getting back to work. Press Secretary James Hagerty asked what he should tell the public.

"Tell the truth," Ike said, "don't try to conceal anything."

So the news was broadcast on television and radio and headlined in newspapers. The president was lying in bed recovering from a heart attack. People in every country were shocked by the news. Americans were afraid. They feared for their country and they feared for the leader they loved.

Mail arrived at the hospital in bundles. After only a few days, there were thousands of get-well letters waiting for someone to open. "I'll answer them," Mamie said. John said later, "I thought she was out of her mind."

But Mamie needed to do something worthwhile during the hours she waited for Ike to regain his strength. So she answered all the letters by hand.

Then came an important question. Would Ike run for office again? Would he be a second-term president?

"Not unless I'm well," Ike told everyone who asked. "Not unless I can be of service to my country."

Eisenhower easily won his bid for reelection.

✑ TEN ✑

Winds of Change

1957-1969

"No man has ever reached his 70th year in the White House ... no man has the faintest right to consider acceptance of a nomination unless he honestly believes that his physical and mental reserves will stand the strain of four years of intensive work."
—Dwight D. Eisenhower

Eisenhower recovered from his heart attack. Once again he campaigned against Adlai Stevenson and won. In his Second Inaugural Address he said, "New forces and new nations stir and strive across the earth. From the deserts of North Africa to the islands of the South Pacific one-third of all mankind has entered upon an historic struggle for a new freedom: freedom from grinding poverty." Across the world, he said, "winds of change" were blowing.

Those winds became Eisenhower's problems.

The Communists were struggling to take control of the Third World. The cold war had spread from Europe to Asia. Decisions about defense, nuclear testing, and civil rights became increasingly urgent. Ike still had to deal with heads of state, generals, and influential persons who wanted their own way.

But there were compensations. The president could enjoy his family. His grandchildren visited the White House often, and John had come to Washington to work with his father.

On October 4, 1957, the Soviets launched the world's first satellite into space. Scientists all over the world marveled at it. Sputnik—the "traveling companion" in Russian—circled the Earth once every 95 minutes.

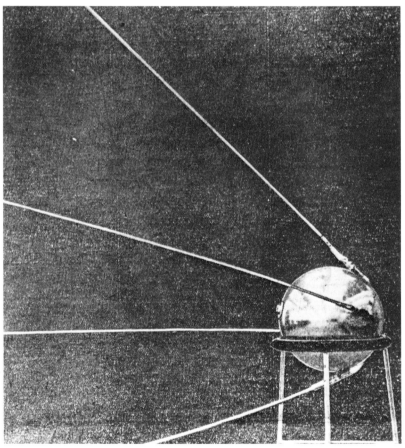

When the Soviets launched the Sputnik satellite, people all over the U.S. were alarmed.

People in the United States were shocked at the news. They worried that the Soviets were ahead in space. Some people blamed the schools. Engineers demanded more money. Army officials were also angry. They said they had a rocket that could have placed a satellite in orbit, but the government had given the space program to the navy. Navy personnel, in turn, were furious. Then the air force became upset. To every department working on the space program, Eisenhower said to stop fighting and start working to get a satellite in orbit.

It didn't take long for the Democrats to blame the Republicans for the lag in space. They did not attack Eisenhower personally—he was too popular for that. But they said his administration was weak. Ike tried to ignore their talk. He had work to do.

Most important on his list of things to accomplish was cutting the cost of defense. He wanted a disarmament program and a ban on nuclear testing. He felt the arms race between powerful nations had to be stopped—but the Soviet Union had to agree.

The Soviet Union was just one of Ike's problems. In the South, civil rights issues continued to flare. In September 1957, in Little Rock, Arkansas, a federal court ordered Central High School desegregated. When nine black students tried to enter, they were threatened with violence. Orval Faubus, governor of Arkansas, used the National Guard to prevent the students from entering. Eisenhower stepped in and put the Guard under federal control and sent an army unit to Little Rock to protect the students.

On the afternoon of November 25, 1957, when Ike went to his desk he suddenly felt dizzy. He could not hold his pen. When he tried to read, the words seemed to run off the top of

In September 1959, Eisenhower met with Soviet leader Nikita Khrushchev, shown here at Camp David.

the page. He tried to stand, but his head swam until he fell back into his chair. His speech was sluggish. After an examination, the doctors said Ike had suffered a stroke.

Ike had promised, "When I cannot serve my country, I will resign." Was this the time? Was he too ill to be president? After recovering, he decided to test his strength by meeting with the heads of NATO. He informed his family that he would fly to Europe.

Ike flew to Paris, wondering what the outcome of the meeting would be. During the meetings, Ike could hold his pen to write and he spoke distinctly. He learned that he could still help world leaders make decisions. As he left, he shook hands with other heads of state. He had passed his test.

For a short while, his work went better. The cold war seemed near an end. In September 1959, Soviet leader Nikita Khrushchev flew to the United States. The Russian dictator traveled around the country, spoke at the United Nations, and went with the Eisenhowers to Camp David. At that time, the two leaders decided to meet the next year in Paris to discuss arms control. The summit was set for May 1960.

Ike looked forward to the summit and he was beginning to trust the Soviet Union. Hopes were high for a thaw in the cold war. But there was one thing lurking in the background that could change everything. Once a month, a U.S. espionage U-2 plane flew over the Soviet Union taking pictures. If the Russians discovered the U.S. spy, Eisenhower would be in trouble.

Ike knew the flights were chancy, but he reasoned that if the Soviets shot down a U-2, they would never admit it. They wouldn't want the world to know they had been spied on for years.

Two weeks before the summit, Ike's telephone rang. He picked it up to hear, "One of our reconnaissance planes, on a scheduled flight from its base in Adana, Turkey, is overdue and possibly lost."

The president hung onto the phone, thinking. He believed the plane was probably destroyed, so there would be no proof of spying. After thinking it over, Eisenhower came to the conclusion that the pilot was dead and the plane had burned. He then tried to cover up the story by announcing to the U.S. public that a plane used for gathering weather information was missing.

The president erred. On a worldwide broadcast, Khrushchev told the news that the Soviet Union had shot down an American spy plane well inside Soviet territory. Khrushchev called it a "bandit flight." He roared that the Americans picked May Day, "the most festive day for our people and the workers of the world, hoping to catch us with our guard down."

The summit was cancelled. The cold war worsened. Hopes for disarmament were gone.

For Eisenhower, work became increasingly difficult, and he worried about the future of the country. Though he promised to finish his term in office, he often thought of retirement. He wanted to fish and play golf. He wanted to spend time with his grandchildren.

During the last months in the White House, Mamie prepared for their move to the farm they had bought in Gettysburg, Pennsylvania. John planned to retire from the army and Ike was offered $1 million for his presidential memoirs.

With Ike's second term almost over, the country was gearing up for another presidential campaign. Nixon would

Eisenhower made a serious error in judgment when he did not tell the U.S. public about the U-2 plane shot down in the Soviet Union. The incident led to a worsening of the cold war.

be a candidate against Massachusetts Senator John F. Kennedy. Ike did not believe that Nixon was ready to run the country, but he wanted him to win. "If the people like what I have done," he thought, "they will vote for the Republican party." The idea of the voters rejecting him and his program made Ike ill.

November 8, 1960, was election day. The Eisenhowers watched the returns on television. Early the next morning, they learned that Kennedy had won. It was one of the saddest days in Ike's life. He blamed himself for the loss. He wondered if there was something he could have done. Ike thought the country was in for heavy spending—spending that he had fought so strongly against.

One morning, shortly before Kennedy was sworn in, Eisenhower stood in the White House Oval Office listening to voices of workers on Pennsylvania Avenue. Hammers pounded. Lumber was being lifted to make a reviewing stand for Kennedy's Inauguration. "Look...," Eisenhower said when an employee entered the room, "it's like being in a death cell and watching them put up the scaffold."

On January 17, 1961, Eisenhower appeared on national radio and television to deliver a Farewell Address to the nation. He spoke of war and peace, of police states, and of freedom. Then the soldier-statesman spoke of his greatest fear—the building of an enormous army. New technology required a huge arms industry, he said. "This conjunction [joining] of an immense military establishment and a large arms industry is new in the American experience. The total influence— economic, political, even spiritual—is felt in every city, every statehouse, every office of the federal government. In the councils of government, we must guard against the acquisition of unwarranted influence, whether sought or unsought, by the military-industrial complex." This complex, he continued, should never be allowed to "endanger our liberties or democratic processes. We should take nothing for granted." He finished by praying that "all peoples will come to live together in a peace guaranteed by the binding force of mutual respect and love."

His words were praised throughout the world.

After retiring from public office, the Eisenhowers lived on their farm near Gettysburg. They owned 260 acres of land and leased an additional 305 acres. There Ike raised hay, corn, oats, barley, soybeans, and sorghum. From his house, he could see fertile green pastures and prize Angus cattle. John and his family lived nearby, so Ike kept horses for his grandchildren to ride and dogs for them to play with.

Then, in April of 1968, Eisenhower suffered another heart attack. The attack was followed by abdominal surgery.

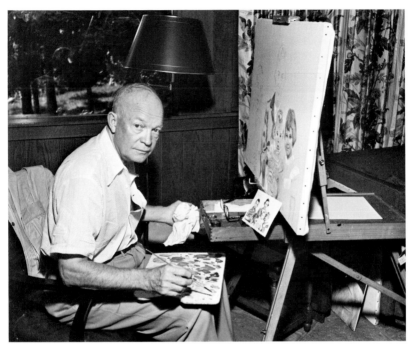

In his retirement, Ike had time for hobbies. One of his favorite pastimes was painting.

By March of 1969, his heart was failing. The end seemed near.

One evening John went to the hospital where his father was staying to say good night. The electrocardiogram machine above his father's bed showed a slight improvement.

"You look better," John said.

Ike was tired. He did not want to talk about what the machine was saying. The next day, March 28, 1969, there was a turn for the worse.

John, David, Mamie, the doctors, and a nurse gathered by Ike's bed.

"Pull me up," Eisenhower told John and one of the doctors.

They lifted him to a sitting position and made him comfortable with pillows. He looked up at his son and smiled.

Then—it was farewell to the boy from Abilene...to the general... to the supreme commander. It was their last "we love you" to the president. "God take me," Eisenhower whispered, and the man called Ike was gone.

A military funeral was held for Eisenhower. His grave is in Abilene, Kansas.

Appendix

Rank (grade) for officers of the U.S. Army

The rank, or grade, system indicates a person's authority and standing in the military. The number of stars on an officer's uniform shows his or her rank. The rank of officers is:

Brigadier General . . . . one star ☆

Major General . . . . two stars ☆☆

Lieutenant General . . . . three stars ☆☆☆

General . . . . four stars ☆☆☆☆

General of the Army . . . . five stars ☆☆☆☆☆

Chief of Staff

A Chief of Staff is a senior officer of the U.S. Army or Air Force. He or she is a member of the Joint Chiefs of Staff.

Joint Chiefs of Staff

The Joint Chiefs of Staff are military advisers to the president of the United States, the secretary of defense, and the National Security Council. They include a chairman, the chiefs of staff of the army, the air force, and the navy. When marine corps matters are considered, the commandant of the marine corps is included. The chairman is appointed by the president and approved by the Senate.

Allies During World War II

Australia
Belgium
Canada
China
Czechoslovakia
Denmark
Ethiopia

France
Great Britain
Greece
India
Netherlands
New Zealand

Norway
Poland
South Africa
Soviet Union
United States
Yugoslavia

Many other countries declared war against the Axis and can be called Allies. The Allies listed above either fought against the Axis with large conventional forces or underground resistance movements, or were occupied by Axis armies.

The Axis

Bulgaria
Finland
Germany

Hungary
Italy

Japan
Romania

Glossary

Allies: the nations united against the Axis powers in World War II.

armistice: an agreement to stop fighting for a long period of time. An armistice often leads to a peace treaty, as the armistice that ended World War I did.

arms race: competition between nations to develop the most powerful weapons; usually refers to nuclear weapons.

Axis: the nations united against the Allied nations in World War II; the three main Axis powers were Germany, Italy, and Japan.

Camp David: the official retreat of the president of the United States. Said to be named for Dwight D. Eisenhower's father and grandson, Camp David lies in a wooded area in Maryland about 70 miles (113 km) from Washington, D.C.

cold war: the struggle between Communist nations and democratic nations that began after World War II. The struggle did not lead to fighting, or "hot" war, so it is called "cold."

Communism: a system of government, based on the ideas of Karl Marx and V.I. Lenin, in which a single authoritarian party controls the nation's means of production.

D-Day: June 6, 1944, the day of the Allied invasion of Normandy, France.

disarmament: limiting, regulating, reducing, or eliminating a nation's weapons and armed forces; also called *arms control.*

French resistance: opposition to the Germans which began in France with the German conquest in June 1940. All types of groups and persons took part in the resistance, which became highly organized.

Front line: the most advanced combat units in a military line.

GIs: United States soldiers.

Great Depression: a period in the 1930s marked by unemployment, business failures, and poverty. The Great Depression followed the stock market crash of 1929 and lasted until 1941, when the U.S. entered World War II.

North Atlantic Treaty Organization (NATO): provides military leadership for the common defense of 16 Western nations. NATO was established in 1950 by the nations that signed the North Atlantic Treaty.

Pentagon: The Pentagon Building in Arlington, Virginia, across the Potomac River from Washington, D.C., houses the Department of Defense of the U.S. government. Built in the shape of a pentagon, or five-sided figure, the Pentagon is one of the world's largest office buildings.

Third World: countries, mainly in Asia, Africa, and Latin America, that have few industries and are poor. Most Third World countries are former colonies of Western European countries. About 60 percent of the people in the Third World live in poverty.

The United Nations: an organization of 159 nations that works for world peace and security and the betterment of humanity. Each nation sends representatives to the UN headquarters in New York City, where they discuss world problems.

whistle-stop campaign: a campaign in which a candidate travels by railroad and speaks to people who gather around the back of the train at each stop along the route.

For Further Reading

BOOKS BY DWIGHT D. EISENHOWER

Eisenhower, Dwight D. *At Ease: Stories I Tell to Friends.*
Garden City, N.Y.: Doubleday & Co., 1967.

———. *Crusade in Europe.* Garden City, N.Y.:
Doubleday & Co., 1948.

———. *In Review: Pictures I've Kept.* Garden City,
N.Y.: Doubleday & Co., 1969.

———. *Letters to Mamie.* Garden City, N.Y.:
Doubleday & Co., 1978.

BOOKS ABOUT DWIGHT D. EISENHOWER

Ambrose, Stephen E. *Eisenhower.* New York: Simon & Schuster,
1983.

Editors of the Army Times. *The Challenge and the Triumph:
The Story of Dwight D. Eisenhower.* New York: G.P. Putnam's
Sons, 1966.

Hargrove, Jim. *Dwight D. Eisenhower.* Chicago: Childrens Press,
1987.

Sixsmith, E.K.G. *Eisenhower as Military Commander.* New York:
Stein and Day, 1983.

BOOKS ABOUT WORLD WAR II

Dank, Milton. *D-Day.* New York: Franklin Watts, 1984.

Graff, Stewart. *The Story of World War II.* New York: E.P. Dutton,
1978.

Marrin, Albert. *Overlord: D-Day and the Invasion of Europe.*
New York: Atheneum, 1982.

BOOKS ABOUT THE PRESIDENCY

Raber, Thomas R. *Election Night.* Minneapolis: Lerner Publications, 1988.

———. *Presidential Campaign.* Minneapolis: Lerner
Publications, 1988.

Samuels, Cynthia K. *It's a Free Country! A Young Person's Guide
to Politics & Elections.* New York: Atheneum, 1988.

INDEX